SIGHING THROUGH GRASSES

Design and Illustrations by Paul Eaton
www.galantedesign.co.uk

Emblem Of The Seeker by kind permission of Jeffrey Kroll
www.krollogy.com

First published in 2011 by Broncroft Books
www.broncroftbooks.jimdo.com

Printed in the UK by Blissetts
www. blissettdigital.co.uk

ISBN: 978-0-9570248-0-9

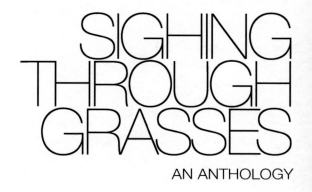

SIGHING THROUGH GRASSES

AN ANTHOLOGY

Maggie Goren
with illustrations by Paul Eaton

Contents

To
The Memory of Michael Stuart

&
to Adam, Matt, Dan and Ben
with love always

"…My eyes were wide open, staring into the dark room, not thinking but feeling all those emotions of love and loss that are the stuff of life, the deep connecting tissue between human beings who are essentially joined and essentially alone."

(From *Going Up, Going Down* by Maggie Goren)

Introduction

It has been suggested that poetry is synthesis, a way of cutting thought to the bone with imaginative, original language responding to innate rhythms of life reflecting every kind of human experience. At its best it is music on the ear, sentience to the heart and precision to the brain…language singing for all the world to hear across time and space.

Somewhere, perhaps, I believe a poem should not have to exceed one line but life is far too complex for that and we could miss so much of the music and meaning! Beyond that, I feel a poet is on a permanent journey; sometimes exhilarating, often disappointing, occasionally getting close to an intended destination.

For many years I was part of a group of a dozen or so people who met regularly in each others' homes to read and enjoy themed poetry from Aristophanes to Auden, Beowulf to James Berry. The volume and variety of poetry was inspirational. Today I still meet three of those lovers of poetry and drama, Annie Hume, Sheila Probert and Nora Wright and greatly appreciate their interest in and comment on my poetry, as well as the enduring friendship we all enjoy.

* * * * *

I am fortunate to have a young friend who has a special talent for tuning into the word with an empathic imagination. As a communicative graphic artist he brings to the poems some remarkable insights with his lovely illustrations. This is a happy symbiosis which enriches my work and gives scope, I would like to believe, to Paul Eaton's own fertile imagination. It has been a great pleasure producing this little book with him.

Maggie Goren, July 2011

Elemental Order

Australasian aborigines requested the sacred bones of their ancestors be returned from a depository in an English museum to their ancestral land, 2003

the dreaming sees
all time as one
no time at all
dancing in circle
round blazing bush fire
air blown down wood
in circular breathing
intoning meaning
from you to me
to you unborn
to you in earth
from me
to you
no end
and no beginning

no need for more
than this

listen to the dawn when
great snake river gods
made sacred life from
water swim and crawl
on land on four on two
to fly and leap
from trees singing
in the wind sighing
through grasses
through sand and stone
in the land
where time began
begins again

for those reborn
for those who listen

man is co-existent
one in
body spirit
life death

in time in timelessness
being all that was
and is

the dreaming

Landscape

Speak to me
in image
not words
break
breakdown
break up
mist over

slower than fire
deep water deep
images of you us

running on
steep cliffs
green soft-piled
rabbit-crossed
sweet gorse-sweet
salt windy
egg-white tossed
sea sun
cloud-cast
shifting shyly
in out
of body touch
warm cool
warm

bright runs the image –
you me
gathering each other
up down
two
one

Birth

The womb weeps her
new offering, her closely
guarded wondrous being,
into his new world…
and loud his cry
as water turns to air
flooding lungs,
while bright lights
stare through
tightly closed eyes,

his tiny legs and fists
flail at the expanding
soft dry space he
feels around him,
until he is placed on
the warm skin of she
whose womb contracted
him into this other
state of being with
pain of love that
words cannot express,
nor need to tell:

mother has been found,
her milky breast is all
that's sweet to you,
sweet miracle.

Swallows

Some of them make it there
and back:
those sleek young things,
neat as waiters used to be,
with no bow-tie but rusty bib,
and fork to tail not hand.

I see one perched on
edge of nest, tail-flap bobbing,
flexing muscle of wing
to fan out ribs in superb,
perfectly sculptured symmetry –
aerodynamic best.

They land on my telephone wires,
measuring a capacity to
balance in the wind,
then swoop in figures of eight to
make a statement of proficiency;
like test pilots they scoop
under the eaves of my car port,
landing with fast precision on
last year's safe house.

They bring huge joy
and awe in natural beauty…
not only for this:

no questions asked,
they do with energetic importance
what instinctively is…

life.

I wish questions did not exist.

Surely I could be happy without them?

Mother

Catapaulting out of bed
to spill the children
into a new day —
hair lathered into submission,
shirts escaping last minute
revision of belt and buckle,
feet knuckled into
double-knotted shoes —
sometimes I feel a proud
but wary ringmaster,
firing his unique cargo
of clown and elephant,
juggler and fire-eater
into an inscrutable crowd —
mantis-faced,
obliquely staring,
praying in the dark
for pleasure,
an appetite for failure
moistening its lips.

Housewife

Failing to find myself
where I'm most likely to be —
juggling with dishes,
pulling laundry from
a moving train —
I peer under the rim of
'A Plain Person's Guide to
Symphony and the Stars' —
and find a galaxy of
unfinished interludes
shooting across my shoulder:
something I strived to fix
in the cross-fire of love
has keeled over.
It might have been me.

Cave Dwellers

Do you think
we are so different…?

cave dwellers in bricks
and mortar,
fires not struck
from sticks but whole trees
buried deep, pick-axed
by men crouched, ranked
in dank, earth-bound tombs —
dark labyrinthine hells that
without warning
cave in…

on warring men
crouched rank in trench,
with stench of fear
and fate
fouling the atmosphere,
beyond the sudden mammoth
sense of stark futility —
without warning…

they too had paintings
on their walls:
cave dwellers bent on
etching immortality in
magic mark on stone —
minds fired to speak,
to reach beyond the possible,
shaft sky and burst
upon the stars
unpiloted ideas…

baggage of hope.

The Sweetest Kiss

Yours was the sweetest kiss –
I knew no others half as sweet
and can't describe the why,
can give no reason, but
yours was the sweetest kiss
under the sky,
in any season.

We were not lovers,
you and I, there
was no treason,
we simply met under
a deep, dark ocean sky,
and set our lips to kissing –
lips parting, lips pressing –

it was a gentle time,
a place for giving,
a taste of fragrance,
ah, such fragrance,
taste of bliss – and,
yours was the sweetest kiss.

Young Woman on Charing Cross Bridge

Propped up and larded in a duvet
smudged with flowers
that Spring had forgotten,
the girl stared at my sweater
smiling, and softly –
'Gorgeous colour, that…
grey-green Irish Sea
on a fair day
gorgeous' – her tousled hair
was dusty red,
she was not begging:

it was its first outing –
to the Hayward –
where Goya's drawings
from his private albums
stopped sudden laughter
in pitiless ink –
unfathomable candour
smudging the edges
of the mind
numb.

'Thank You'…I said brightly
to the girl on the bridge,
as though she'd gifted it
from her own hand –
and kept on walking,
wondering if I might have…?

reaching The Strand,
I wept a little…
for Goya,
the girl
and me.

The (Glyptotek) Carlsberg Heads of Roman Emperors

Thank you, Mr. Carl Jacobsen,
not for heads of beer
but heads of men,

lifesize, lifelike,
like life indeed,

just like the headmen, despots
of another year, today,
tomorrow;

fine figures and faces
I might borrow
to fit a few shoulders
well-known in high places:

so close I get in the gallery
that I can read stone lips,
stare into stone eyes,

observe, with ambling ease,
a cruel stone mouth,
a broken nose of stone,
brow stonily creased;

ambition, pride, madness, query,
seek through sightless eyes
their stony destinies…
wild fire of victory, dirt of defeat:

yet gladly, indeed, I also see
compassion, tenderness,
fear, need:

Sirs! zoo-trapped, unmoveable
under your own steam, you
   cross
time and history for arguable
   review,
and petrified toss our talking
   heads
into those deep, unfathomable
   wells
of hope and loss.

Ambivalence

It is the falling
between things that
hurts the mind:

the song-thrush with
his miracle calling
is altogether
more purposeful,
more knowing,
as he tosses
from his throat a
string of glass beads
to rise and fall,
translucent, glowing,
let loose in circular cadences
upon a world disrobed
and waiting;

while I, with
breath abating
till he cease his
song or flies,
descend into a
state of mind that
cannot take in
such incredible beauty
without crying.

Had You Come Back Differently

Had you come back differently –
though I did not expect you
to appear with a rose
between your teeth –
but with jacket not buttoned oddly,
with something matching in
shirt and tie,
without handkerchief
bulging in pocket…

I might have seen something new
in the you who went away,
reviewed my feelings,
turned a blind eye to old habits,

but as chance would have it,
absence had not slowed you down
on a Damascus road,
pouring new light on
an old relationship…
life-changing stuff like that,

and why should it?
I too remain much the same…

well, I've been thinking,
maybe absence is the thing,

like travelling hopefully.

Penelope

You won't get away
with being simply
the woman who waits day by day
for a decent return on loyalty:

I know you have been
spinning a good yarn
over twenty years
that had its beginning
on the sheep's back and belly,
keeping her pregnantly warm
through storm dark winter till
Spring let down the lamb;

softly you sing an old song
'he said he'd come
when cherry bloom
had lengthened on
the speckled bough,
and so he came' –
you have your son.

I see you more
at the quiet centre of
full-centred being –

seasons abhor a vacuum:
spring flowers wreathe your
gold-flecked hair, wakening desire,
you watch darting swallows return
to last year's nests,
deep dawn of harvest warms you,
November's first fires burn,

and so the years turn,
and if your door swings open
    now
upon an asylum of noisy suitors –
well, you hold the key;

beauty and power walk hand in
    hand –
and there's pleasure to be had in
    that:

cold sea slams up against the
    shore
empty of ships,
empty of promise,
Laertes' shroud shrinks,
will not be finished,
time's text dissolves;

I think, my lady, you are
    content…
until…let's see what happens
    next…
what continents unfold…

Caged Freedom

Inspired by Jonathan Harvey's music composition '*Scena*'

You grind against the bars,
metallic sound mounting
from a rumble to
to an iron chord as the
strings of your voice rise
keening, wailing to
a fine, high pitch
that ends beyond hearing,
breaching the solid walls,
escaping as any spirit might,
defying iron and stone,
flying like a vision, like a dream,
to certain freedom
beyond the prison of the mind –
cage that is yours alone:

suddenly the lion roar,
woodwind hesitates as
base takes up the score, the
trembling tune, rushing,
descending again to the floor
where with eyes wide open you see,
not the white space without bars
for flying through
but the white coats coming,
running to open the clanking door
and hold you in their arms,
needle poised to loose
your fears…that just now
flew on angel wings.

At The Water's Edge

Your movement in the water,
beyond your will but beautiful,
edging in towards the shingle,
swept out on a sliding tide,
dissolved uncertainty:

you were young and you had
   died,
that morning only?

Water was your element now,
not sky,
which had seen you briefly
since cracking the shell,
wheeling, crying, swooping down
with the hellish crowd for
the day's pickings, raucous,
voracious, loud, believing
that was all there was to it –
no, not quite all – the instinctual
sharp-eyed fear was near,
ready for take off.

You could not know nor care
how beautiful you were,
before death's deep
   disintegration,
as a light swell lifted your wings
in ovation to seeming life
on balletic tidal rhythms,

gently out, then in against your
feather plump,
brown-pencilled breast,
feet down pointing,
your slender neck softening
   slowly
to a curved arch, your head
swaying to rest first one side,
then the other,
with classical precision;

yours was a soft, a watery
   crucifixion –
no nails, no tearing of flesh, no
   storm,
no crying out – just a quiet
   moment's
tender benediction.

Falling Stars

Poem specially written for a musical composition by Dan Goren, performed by 'The Sixteen' in the Jacqueline du Pré Music Building, Oxford, 2006

How many stars fell
from the sky that night,
and fell and fell
like rain,
like fireworks
to blaze and die –
and no-one seemed
to mind or care
to search to find
the place on which
they lay spent
of their brilliance –
or did they pass
the rim of earth
to sink in space
from whence they came
with spies perhaps
to spy on us
in borrowed light
and time and silence:

or did they fall,
down dash
without a splash
into the wide
Atlantic deep
Sargass…
Sargasso Sea,
into its wheeling
waving weed and
through to deepest
Caribbean blue –
or maybe drop

their fire off
Friendly Islands'
Bora Bora's
turquoise waters,
Raiatea and Moorea,
just to light
their deeps at night
with shining,
shining bright.

You were…

the sea on which I sailed
without a compass,
believing in the true North,
the mouth of the river
wider than my imagining,
the desert
island of no return.

You could not stop
to weigh anchor and lie down
in the mouth of the moon,
to stare at stars without a future,
to leave words alone
and fold yourself
into peace —
to be nothing.

You issued from another land
where time has run out,
and groaned your way back
into broken dreams:
you were the prophet
without portfolio,
bedazzled by your own words
into self authenticating,
folding like paper
into no new shape,
your canny hieroglyphs
disintegrating into dust.

You could not stop
for love,
which has no destination,
no tangible geography,
no time —
of doubtful existence.

Moon Unexpected

Suddenly, there is this peachy
dinner plate of a moon
edged with a fuzzy fringe
of creamy muslin,
hanging there, so near the ground,
right outside my window,

so huge is she, so close,
so lunaversal, so bound to be
in the hands of the magician
just like his other showy trappings
on a darkened stage,
and thus she casts a deep spell
of anticipation with her circle of light,
attending his will;

breath held, I wait,
knowing in seconds only
my dinner plate moon,
more beautiful than
Sèvres or Wedgwood,
could, if I take my eyes off her,
spin beyond control to fly
orbital in the September sky
smaller than a saucer…

and so it happens…

stage magician fades
from the scene…

but magic moon I will remember.

Amsterdam (Hot July, 2005)

Vondelpark has its magpies too,
and litterbugs and men
with tattooed arms and legs,
bikes and cameras galore
and sore, sunburnt bellies and
    busts.

We are a stones-throw,
pigeon's coo,
from art lovers' lusts –
the Ryjks Museum,
Vincent's holy shrine,
the Staedlijk, closed for
overdue refurbishment,
its 'moderns' under dust covers,
while elsewhere 'would-be-
    goods'
exhibit guns and crap and snot
and tired pop art,
for lack of skill and shine
or 'lust for life'…?
they should be so lucky
for God's sake…

…perhaps not!

There seems a calm here,
easy-going charm,
a sky that's not oppressed
with too much traffic noise and
    smoke –
far cry from the grime beneath
    the nails,
the sucked in cheeks, the
    pouting mouths
and deep, dark hungry eyes
of the 'Potato Eaters' –

masterstroke of a man
with belly full enough
but little hope of attracting
    attention:

Van Gogh's 'image' lingers,
and the heat:
a storm's predictable,
grumbles in my mind –
nothing to mention really –
but in my heart, Vincent,
a curious, missed beat.

Flying Girl

Image, Vietnam 1972, of child running from napalm bombing;
subsequent meeting, 2010, of reporter Christopher Wain with
Kim Phúc

Flying girl,
angel child with arms
wide stretching out
to sky
from where no
help comes,

only the deep-hell heat,
skin-burning cry,
while in one
brief blink
a camera's eye shuts,
shifts and blinks again
at the searing scene.

Astonishment will not recoil
until a world-wide press
is read, the image seen…

…is that child dead, they ask?

One reporter saw
with live astonishment;
the camerman giving his
    support,
they caught the flying child
and straightway poured cold
water on her lips and skin…
sealed her fate.

* * * *

For years you flew
from that mad image,
its politics and pain…
but it ran after you.

Finally, you caught up;
so now you plant
your pain, your fear
(on still scorched earth)
with softly spoken words
for worldwide ears to hear…

your talk's of hope, of love…

but do they listen…?

pain, largely, is indifferent
to those who do not bear it.

Darkness Approaches Lindisfarne

To Viv, my good and trusty travelling companion

A gash across the sky,
blood red seeping
into old gold sea
sporting silvered seal,
flash of white as a
single tern clips
a dash of spray,
the short-eared owl calling.

Blood red seeping
into monkish grey
and bowed black back
of priest exalting God,
Cuthbert by name,
who lay down in his cell
but did not die
as other men do.

Lying close with his God
he slept eleven years
to stare back undespoiled
into the eye of the despoiler
of his simple, chosen grave
on Farne Island.

They carried him over track
and ditch and fell and scree
till all the flesh dropped off
his bones, over rocks
and hills and stony paths
until one day they found a box
for his bones to rattle in;

no resting place for
this saintly man who
gave his life to his fellowmen,
then wishing only

to die in peace,
to lie in peace
where sky and wind
and sea greet God
on a level field, horizonless,
on Farne Island.

Was that a tearing wind
crying to those who
did not listen, did not hear
sweet Cuthbert's prayer:

'I am not here, not here
but everywhere and blessed
is he who sleeps forever
in peace in his chosen place:
my bones are dust
and meaningless to all
who would chase eternity in
a physical space carved out
by the powerful few,
who would use
those bones as talisman,
celestial charm, to turn
away the devil, smile on God,
and hold you to a masquerade:

hear me in the wind and rain,
the wave, the drifting snow,
and know no power on earth,
in heaven, resides in bones,
has breath,
but only the spirit that flies
beyond both life and death
can bear you boundless
into that everlasting, deep,
sweet unity you crave'.

Remembrance Sunday 1980

To the memory of my grandfather, killed in battle, 1918

Every year it is the same,
Autumn melting on the pavements,
A mild astonishment that weather
Could be so suitably grey,
No mourning in the trees,
But for chance lightning –
Act of God –
They drop their leaves naturally.

Every year it is the same,
The inexplicable sorrow falling
Like snow on the old olives
And the green age hawking
Among her gnarled roots –
Act of God –
Until the Spring shoots.

Every year it is the same,
Cold tears spilling into hearts
From vast seas of graves
Rolling in a deafening quiet
Along our numbed nerves,
Hurting our foolishness
Into self-forgetting –
Act of faith –
Where deeper homage serves.

I walked amongst you once
At Arromanche,
The air so still
I hardly dared to breathe –
It seemed just then a sacrilege
To stare and turn away,
For part of me is there
In you, in this day
Which is all my days.

Taking The Children
To The Family Service

Be thankful, then —
and let the children bless
with unconcern,
this average union,
which raised them to flower
in a wilderness...

but await no pardon
when in time they stray
beyond the lychgate,
and too soon display contempt
for our mean measure of success,
our poverty of mind —

we may also find that day
our less than perfect union
under scrutiny...

pause for redress...

they too, one day,
may come to the same service.

On Being Alive

Why am I buzzing
around this business
of being alive –
it's so short-lived
after all?
I could obliterate
the racing thought,
put out those
lightning strikes
of memory
and "just be" –
as old Ma Neal
once said.

And why not?

Because, I guess,
it's something else,
being alive,
undead,
like humdinger singing
from rafters,
like feeling the crying,
the heartbreak,
the healing touch,
laughter's deep cleansing,
the sharing, the loving –
and simply knowing you
are not yet in that
weedy plot –

heady stuff,
thrilling!

Fig Trees

A fig tree hangs over
my garden wall
to remind me of a
garden I once knew
in Israel, where
winds of war
blew hot, blew cold,
blew out, blew in;

reminds me too
of paradise,
of Omar Khayam
under those boughs
with book and wine
and his beloved,
and when I once
stalked history,
walking in beauty
among fig trees
by water gardens
of the Alhambra.

Life is moving
history as I write:
and in its thin
continuous thread
I see the many mes
who made me
back to Eve,
who weeps,
is always weeping,

and in my head
thought stumbles
recklessly across
millennia of
stubble fields,
where morning mists

curl up in vapour wreaths
mourning men laid down
in battlefields,
in wars never so
glorious as they
were meant to be:

their bloodied bodies
sown into the earth
the whole earth over,
their bones ploughed
in by shares
to feed the
next year's corn,

and big bellied Eve
lies weeping still
beneath the fig tree.

The earth is round
so there can be
no ends to it,
no sacred fields,
no heroes,
no Elysium.

I pick a fig
from the branch
hung over my wall;
it is purple like
old blood,
scented, warm,
soft to touch,
glorious to eat;

I am not young,
I am too tired
to weep.

Instant Mozart

The wind picks furiously at
last leaves, determined
to lay them down on the ground,
rain spits out of dull grey cloud
and spits and spits all day,
I sit before autumnal flame of a
full fire burning brashly in the
   grate,
well fed, warm…

press a button…

instant genius, instant Mozart,
violin and piano sweet as victory,
Barenboim and Perlman,
instant heroes:

later, maybe, I'll hear Maria,
outstanding Callas, as the mad,
the dying Lucia…
at the press of a button…

and cry cosily:

instant pizza from Marks &
   Spencer,
chocolate cake, wine or beer,
TV news, I can choose the
   channel

for scenes as raw as the mad
   Lucia,
savage as man or nature can be,

flick a switch and still I see
too many pressed into hapless
   life,
swept into war, disease, famine,
despotic cruelty, hopeless fear…

I switch off…

no pause, no switch-off,
no choice for them,

no place, it would seem,
for instant genius?

So, one small plea…a little
   grace…
'dear Lord and Father of
   mankind'…

however Mozart came to me

let him come by any means,
sound, sight, touch, love,
   whatever…

if for an instant only…

to my unfortunate sister and
   brother.

Otherness

You are another,
don't you see,
other than me;
skull barrier but more –
a door that fails to open
to the spoken word,
alarms within to ward off
unsolicited gifts of arms,
in case they pierce your skin.

Wooden, discreet you
rock upon your hinges
to absorb the shock
of boot or fingertip or even
lip pressed to the lock,
in short, to resist defeat:

yet groaning still
for such there is in you,
in I, in otherness my love,
that mourns its flesh
which so entailed
in self-containing will,
cannot yet fly into
another being and,
becoming one, identify.

A personal view of the extraordinary paintings of the New York, abstract artist, **Jeffrey Kroll**. Plato said: *"The painter makes a dream for those who are awake"*

exploding light whirling
through cut diamond
bright to dark
holding the frame
light contained yet
free as air

tempered strokes of
brush rag rule
empowered to fool time

tight black and white
diffused to nano degree
of infinite colour unfolding
infinite form in space dynamic
to core stillness

rainbow light arced
spliced
showering the sight the mind
in volcanic sparked
dark purple vivid scarlet
midnight pink light
spilling in rough eruption
to smooth lakeside
green blue back
to black white stillness

time unframed

mind aware
deeply dreaming in
wakefulness intensified
seeing beyond the frame
mysterious evolving being

flying free as air

Spring Tide

Is this the point of no return:
penultimate view
after long-time staring
hurt the eyes,
burned out the mind,
when reaching out to you
brought this much understanding
and no more…
that you and I move like the sea
upon each other's alien shore?

That we would cover all our lands
with an inward surge of tides
is not denied;

huge oceans pull us out
and break us short…
the shingle slides.

The Photograph

To Sheila with love, August 2011

My friend took
a photograph of me
trying to be what I am not…
a star, someone heroic,
sad or simply stoic,
a lady lost in history,
a woman of mystery
standing on the end
of a wall out to sea,
the 'cobb' they call it.

Well, she tried very hard
but somehow, I feel,
anxiety got in the way
of the shot or maybe
it was just that she
couldn't see in the viewer,
what with a high sun
poking its rays straight at her,
the wind blowing hair
in her eyes or the fact that
it was a new camera,
more simply put, perhaps
she was not that interested
in the plot,
whatever…

of course, she could have been
standing too high, too low,
too close to the wall,
too far, too near or was she
too early, too late…but really
all of this makes
no difference whatsoever
to the picture, in which I appear
headless,
cut off at the neck,
statuesque to a degree, I grant you,
but headless:

the wall nevertheless seems
firm enough, noble even,
its curved barricade snaking
out to sea with
no other pretension than to act
as protection for the harbour,
its bobbing boats, the landing
   stage,
a tangle of nets:

no doubt it will feature in
thousands of spectacular photos,
in sun, wind or rain…

but it's doubtful if ever
we'll go there again.

Time In

For my granddaughter, Ruby, aged five

Your hair is honey silk,
Your blue eyes shine with no
Untimely knowledge,
Your skin as cream on milk,
Your blush, your tears,
Your little fears reside
For seconds only,
And resign;
You are lively and well
And know no ill
My darling dove,
For you are only five…
And innocence and love,
Love, love, enfold you still.

For my granddaughter, Zahra, aged four

Your hair is warm earth, curly,
Your eyes, dark as the deep well,
Shine with brightness of mind,
Your will is adamant and yet
You fold yourself so sweetly
Into a soft submission,
Like a sprite you dart here and there
On fast, light limbs,
Giggling with mirth,
Your voice sings truly on the ear
My dear, sweet heart…
There is no thing on earth
You cannot bring into the arms
Of the loving ring around you.

Time Out

For old me

Life has run in circles
round my years
so that my wonder grows:

I find that what began
upon the fiddler's strings
in rambling tunes
when I was young,
has followed on and,
faint or strong, just like
the rose in flower and thorn,
returns upon a season;

yet it may also be that
love, laughter, tears,
shake out their leaves
from dead diaries
to fall in magic circles
round those years,
shielding me softly from
misread memory,
uncouth reason:

so now is the time
to settle in circles,
to the singing of bow
on the fiddler's strings those
life-arching melodies
from long ago,
and I'll laugh with sun rising
and dance down the dawn
till day is done...
let love live or go.

Portrait of W. H. Auden

The ridge and furrow
of your heavy face
went up in smoke

you were a bloke
fallen from grace
for leaving your place
on fire with incendiaries
to stalk the snowy
sidewalks of New York

other conscientious fellows
put out the burning
buildings with hose
and pails of water
or *came out*
and sat in jails

but the limestone poet
ridge and furrow
hill and dale
walked still in your
green valleys
spinning words trite
as doggerel
or dense with meaning
as your gargoyle head
or interchangeable

so you returned
were heard in Oxford
given grace
and weight
and read

in autumn years
your bonfire was
piled high with fallen leaves
damp with uncertainties
its pace of burning
fuelled with wit
its ashes blazing
with outstanding words

Neanderthal

Poor fellow,
they're still raging
over your pedigree,
your right to
a lounge suit and
free entrance to
the Club of
Modern Man —
no bouncer to decree
that occipital bun,
that heavy brow,
receding chin and
forward face,
a strict sartorial ban:

and if you petered out
because flat heads
were not such fashionable fun
as the high, millennium-domed
skull of Homo sapiens sapiens,
whose tongue flew down
his throat and was
his sharpest asset…
next to his sexy
linear line and spear…
all that Out of Africa gear —

just don't feel bad
'our man from the valley' —
we know you cared,
shared food in life,
in death strewed flowers:
and, if by chance
a wandering lass
did meet her doom with
Homo sapiens sapiens,
caved up with him,
settled the argument
with a gene or two
(the best tonic)…
then Who's Who?

I ask you…!

The Kiss

Inspired by a photo of Rodin's 90 years' old model, Victor

Newspaper cutting from the
   fifties
wedged between pages of
reconstructed art, smart and
   glossy
under covers of the Phaidon
   Press;
you stand beside the statue
fully dressed,
your sad clothes hanging from
the big bone structure
(light in flesh now with the
dark passing of years)
stooped rather than bent over
the fluid form you kissed
to world acclaim and
critical accord for the sculptor.

I'm moved to wonder
where your thoughts
and feelings flow;
how you can view this stone,
this pale and monumental ghost
hewn from your own youth –
that yet surprises and delights,
in its surpassing beauty,
hidden aspirations in hearts
of most men and women,
young and old alike?

Was your commitment ordinary
   then –
a pose for pennies to redress the
   cold,
and satisfy a hunger less pretentious
than that of bold critics stealing
across galleries of bronze and
   stone
in search of gold?

You peer into the lens
of a photographer
in urgent haste,
who snaps you
for a few francs
and curiosity value –
that some distracted editor
might mount you in a space
he cannot fill with more disaster
or political complaint.

And still I'm moved to wonder
where your thoughts
and feelings flow:
without you Rodin had no mind,
perhaps, to press his artistry;
you were the living link,
the leading lines to the soul
he wished with loving skill
to chisel out –
your bone and fibre all
of nature's mystery to him.

Whatever you may think,
old man,
whatever tears or laughter
have disturbed
your petty wanderings,
whatever kisses left their print
upon a mouth
as lovingly inclined as hers –
no other kiss could burn you
into immortality
like this.

Border Badlands

In Memory of 'Little' Adam, 1985 – 2006

The tank – a scaly,
antediluvian beast,
decked for deceit –
lumbered into the
still night landscape:

Chinese ink and water,
tranquil, waiting,
stripped to essentials;
moonlit, misted, brushed
in ochre and black,
sky, stark at a stroke,
hanging there,
solid back of beast a mere
smudge on grassless terra firma:

turret, gun, infrared eye
seeking its crippled mate,
rumbling across deadlines
and hate, its four man crew
alert in Trojan silence
in the dark underbelly:

they said it could not be
entered through the side
(unlike cold steel piercing the
flank of one who died for love
in ancient Israel) – its head
    and tail
alone were vulnerable:

so through the tail
the rocket came
in no time at all,

no time to clear
the throat of fear
or lose hope,

no time at all
for the dispersal
of flesh to a different
configuration of atoms
that cannot be kissed,

no time to hurt even,

as if nothing human
had been, as if grief
did not exist.

Prayer For
A Fallen Soldier

For Aliza & Yigal

They have stopped your song –
The Song of Life.

They have given you silence
Which cannot be broken.

They have broken hearts
Which cannot be mended.

They have taken your age
And left us finite youth –
A gift too cruel, too devastating.

They have halted time and space
For we who mourn
As helpless crying babes
Your youth, your love, your Song.

God give us grace this day
To know what They do not –
And hold this son of ours
Within your love, forever.

יי לא אמות כי אחיה ואספר מעשי יה: ...

From Psalm 118:17

Black And White

Black and white
up and down
left and right
night and day
you can fix it
it either way
inside out
outside in
there's the flesh
here's the skin
here's the virtue
there's the sin
something firm
something stout
for all of us
to shout about.

They make rules
rules are fun
black and white
every one
only fools
dark glasses on
look at the sun
miss the firing
of the gun
miss the bright
the right solution
only one.

Here's the truth
there's the lie
makes life easy
till you die
so they say

but my heart
tugs at my mind
to escape
this double bind

wants the comfort
wants the doubt
wants to let
the whole truth out
running on its
liquid way keeping
black and white
at bay

in ever flowing
shades of grey.

Jerusalem

At the extreme ends
or centre
of thinking,

you draw men to
a vision that
extends
and betrays
their humanity,
drop by little drop
in blood or holy water:

you are fire
from middle earth
cracking the surface,
light that flies faster
than man can grasp,
though he sees it passing
with every new dawn:

consumed yourself by fire
not once, not twice
but on and on…
you will defy
stark mortality
to be re-born
upon the same hill…

for each of us
dying to the dark,
once only.

On looking at Rembrandt's Portrait 'The Old Jew'

(c. 1660s) at the Hermitage, St. Petersburg

Centuries cloud your eyes;
an old rheum
that adds its personal mist
to lies and truths
confused now in a
history of griefs.

What was your youth?
Did Mama tell you tales
that raised your hair on end,
and did you run from them
in certainty that bookish things
would give you cunning
to outwit the worst of men?
And your dark beauty,
pride, pretend a
conquering of every fair
in finery and rings?

And did you learn, young man,
to pick the pockets of the rich
in market squares,
legitimately?
To add too soon to
your vocabulary of mind,
that mulish burden,
dark inheritance of self deceit,
that you are chosen, an elite,
to make of guilt
a martyrdom for other men.

And did you love and lose
and like and hate
and bow before that
age-old fear of difference
with smiles and gestures?
Did you abdicate your
public self respect
in private honour of
a Jewish fate?

Old Jew, I stand before you now
with hindsight horrible,
your future set in deaths
man can't redeem:
your rheumy eyes convey
a message still to me,
captured by that old master
of compassion –
strangely, you seem unsurprised.

The Thin People

I say we are thin
as a fly's wing,
crushable to
tattered lace
in no time at all;

of course it is no sin
to be ninety-three –
but not a huge honour
either, simply an
act of grace, if so
you wish to see it,
to be in this place
where air is cheap
and memory too much
a forgotten thing…

but none of it
matters really;
living, being, doing,
loving, dying even…

so, I ask you,
what is important…
nothing?

Well, you tell me,
after a pause,
each day we
may laugh and
be curious –
for nothing!…

deo volente!

Pregnant Egyptian Queen

Bronze by Nadin Senft

Striding across dynasties,
your regal elegance
proclaims a new Sun God,
as though fecundity were all —
ignoring the shot in the dark to murder death,
despair, stark disbelief —
bearing this time, maybe, the grasp of genius,
compassion's cope, unquenchable fire
to force the heavens apart
for light:
your bright, firm strength of purpose
giving back
life for life,
love for love,
hope for hope.

Four Sons

I have four sons –
Isaac, Joseph, Joshua, Benjamin –
their names are legend,
father, Abraham:

they, on the other hand,
are like most boys –
cheek the teacher,
choke on a fag,
dream of girls and motorbikes
and knowing all the answers –
pretend to study.

Each name beats an echo
that winds up with the wind
round the hills of Judea
down to the desert,
where vultures spiral
almost out of sight
searching for the killed –
dark smudges on the
clean sheet of sky.

My boys skate ramps,
scream at rock concerts,
sometimes fight each other,
grow up and dare not
tell their mother much,

their names compound
the cantor's lament,
the call of the muezzin,
the cry from the cross:

my sons have sons now
of their own –
don't want to hate,
don't want to kill
each other
in no man's land –
where vultures circle still –

if God or Allah will it.

A Precious Thing

I have no time to
keep a vigil on
the world's woes,

to step up to
the empty table
knowing I cannot
replenish it,

to weep a salt lake
dead from the beginning,

time is a precious thing;
I must make
my daily communion
with the sun,

bathe in the hours
of light,
speak in the tongue
I have been given
to my children's
children,

but with innocence
and laughter,
avoiding places in
our vocabulary that
would admit…

a world's woes,
the life and death of it:

time hereafter is time enough
to sit
and sadly sing in the shadows,

time now is a precious thing.

Skopelos

Rain falls on Skopelos
and Eden rises from the ground
in pungent smell of figs,
soaked earth and pines,
reeking of genesis.

I am reminded, somehow,
recognise the scent
of time eclipsed;
essential languor,
heat-hazed reason,
the old seasonal round
of birth, life, death entwined
in timeless naturalness.

You are not here –

here in this Eden's garden
where first we met,
well dressed
in innocence and awe,
until, like all our kin,
we fell
to taste the dust
of Eden's promise:

and yet, somewhere beyond
our earthy longings,
small beginnings, smaller endings,
fruit of forgetfulness will ripen,
sweet opiate of Paradise
for you and I who mixed and
    made
of our desires a waking dream,
a mad nightmare,
a comic union.

Rain falls on Skopelos
and drowns, drowns, drowns
    the sun
in soft life-giving fellowship:

you are not here –

and all of this, it seems to me,
is one.

First Only Love

I wonder why I think
of the loss of you
still,
from a perspective
almost astronomical…

from the far end of a telescope
sweeping the heavens for
one distant star
at its dead, dark centre:

why I wonder is
my eye still fixed on a far field,
a foreign night sky
alight with a trillion stars above,
where
head bowed, I kneeled
on hard, unfeeling earth and
rocking with arms
tight crossed at breast,
wept, wept, wept for
love lost…

love that had surely died and yet,
with all that weeping done for
a dead star streaking
still
through time and space…
is never laid to rest.

Language

Language is a convenience:

how else could I tell you
that the tree bent down
and whispered in my ear
of murder,

how the sea bellowed
of greed and the scrape
of her womb, leaving
dead fish flying in the air,

how the sun shouted, laughing,
'beware, I am not here forever,
worship me and you will burn out
with me',

how time giggled and
pointing at the me-tic-ulous
movement of the clock
shrugged, with infinite grace:

how else could I tell you

time and silence
hear the tree,
listen to the ocean
smile at the sun?…

words are, for the most part,
for you and me,
a mere, haphazard convenience.

Gien Vase

Remembering Gwen

Friend, you left me
a tall and comely ceramic vase
conforming tenderly to woman;
neck rising to open
with generosity,
shoulders sloping down
in elegant curve to slender waist,
hips softly tapering to a neat base
planted firmly on the ground:

the flourishing pattern,
deep gold on deeper blue
of the traditional Gien pottery,
strongly resembles your beauty,
and rising out of it I sense
the essence of you:

respected, revered,
and loved by many men,
who gave you sway
without demand,
and I in awe of that,
who could not dream
to even such a score:

you were woman in the
timeless sense of knowing
timeless man, understanding
his constant need for care,
attention, flattery,
his fear of losing face…
losing the smallest thing, indeed,
that gives him place,
your place beside him even…

but 'just remember, if you love
    him,'
said she, 'he is only a man…
not king, not potentate nor god,
heaven forbid,
and it is pointless to blame him
for anything,
whether there is right in it or no,
for he is only a man
who has no wish, you see, to
    listen to
or understand a woman.'

I smile now, remembering how
I once called you
'handmaiden' but you it was
who played the better hand,
received the better deal,
you who were the wiser
of we two…and yet…

I smile again, remembering
love also bound you
to his scourging, velvet wheel.

The Strongest Link

Life is fragile
like tissue paper
wrapping a flimsy thing,
like ice when sun rises,
or glass palaces we
inhabit now and then,
like the poem of a child
describing dew on the grass,
like anything you care
to mention really,
including you and me –
fragile:

but letting that pass,
we all make a stab
at being…something…
printing our thumb's
original landscape on
an old, old scene:
fathers, mothers, artists,
scientists, poets, lovers…

comedians perhaps
are the most fragile,
most important
of women and men,
and the strongest link
establishing direct
connections in chains
of laughter back to
the beginning when
we stood for the first time,
peeping over the tall
grasses of the savannah,

blinking at our audacity –
laughing.

An Old Maid

I remember Miss Moreton,
stern and stringy,
grey hair in a bun,
who taught us history
at the all girls school.

She was tall,
her voice precisely soft
but firm, no-one would
dare to mess around
in her class,
she could pre-empt such
foolishness with a stare
that shrank you down
to status of clown
or idiot before the thought
was even there:

until…until one day
she stood in for
our English teacher
taken ill…
and gave herself away.

"Open your poetry books"
she said "at page
one hundred and eleven",
and picked on me to read.

"When you are old and grey
and full of sleep"…I began
…*"take down this book…"*

At fourteen love was surely
in the air, more surely on
the brain, and I was
quite aware of Mr Yeats'
unrequited love for Maud
and this great poem;

I read on to the last verse…

"Murmur, a little sadly, how Love
fled…"

glancing up briefly to see
Miss Moreton dreaming
over my head into some
misty middle distance,
like a young wife gazing
across a rough sea for sight
of her fisherman,
sailor home from the wars…

I finished
"And paced upon the mountains
overhead
And hid his face amid a crowd of
stars"

a tiny pause, then,

"Thank you Margaret, please sit
down,"
was all Miss Moreton said.

Lines from W. B. Yeats's poem 'When You Are Old'

This Instant

Out of a bomb site,
a weed grows,

out of a hurt heart,
love grows:

life forced through
hairline cracks by
an exploding seed's
refusal to lie dormant…

the strength of will
to believe against
all odds
that love is…

are kinds of miracle;

but that their sight,
scent, touch is how
they move me now…
this instant…
is all that matters,
all that's meant.

Daily Express

BLITZ BOMBING OF LONDON
GOES ON ALL NIGHT

The Line

There is a line
like the horizon,
which does not exist,
between you and me.

It may be curved
and taut like a bow
for all I know,
or straight
but indeterminate.

The fact is the
closer we sail
towards it, as we think,
is mind-miraging only;
the line keeps its distance
as close to exact as
the single atom of a
billionfold on the point
of a pin...

and yet this distance defines
the essential you and me –
not to be reached in ships.

Judas Tree (Israel 1973)

We hear him coming down the
   lane,
the children wonder,
sometimes stare to see
the old white-headed man
with hat pulled down against the
   glare,
tap-tapping gently past our lives
with his thin Malacca cane.

The fiscal compensation
buys him bread,
but what of pain?
No change exists
that can alleviate
the dull, hard drumming in his
   brain,
the memory that beats its wings
behind the bolted shutters of
   his mind
by day, and waits with sick intent
to prey upon his dreams with
night's swift liberation.

Just once I heard the thick night
   air
split into a thousand fragments
with his scream –
and ran like Mother Fury
to the room where my young
   children
lay in peace –
and stood aghast and shook
at the raw vision of his dream:

An open door,
   The uniforms,
     The guns,

A madman viced
in brawny arms,
howling as they centred on
his own life's blood.

Esther six,
   Hannah ten,
     The loving Ruth,
three children huddled close
against the inexpungeable
barbarity of men,
and from this deepest well
of innocence
one cry,
again and yet again,
   Father!
     Father!

A volley spent,
the scarred wall
of a cell stands dumb –
and silence as
three
   petals
     fell,
softly now
in deepest pink
at Spring's ending.

I Do Love

I do love
this terrible, sad world
in which we live;
its people rich and poor,
its children, come what may,
its cats and dogs and elephants,
its threatened species —
dare I say like us —

the fuss we make in politics
to break even, to break free,
to season the salt of corruption
with sweeteners of justice:

I do love
this terrible, sad world
that lies open in her beauty
like a woman,
whom love or hate can enter
and lay waste —
or make more beautiful.

Earthquake In The Midlands, 2000

She left a message
on the answer-phone:
'It's over,
it won't work.'
She seemed breathless –
the tone of her voice
then crisped, levelled
to shoulder height and
with rifle precision fired
'We're dead.'
in face of the absent enemy,
me.

I cried as though
I'd been hit
'No, you can't do this,
not this way,
it's cowardice,
not fair play,
not fit,
not civilized' –
the phone purred.
I banged my fist
on the table,
the chairs shook,
nattering to one another,
legs tut-tutting as
I pushed past and stumbled
up the stairs.

That night the bed shook –
disturbed and in anquish
I turned to emptiness
and lay hard breathing
before pulling the blanket
over my head:

next morning, 'it was
an earthquake', they said.

Seeming Age

Your seeming age erects no boundaries,
no picket lines to keep the past out,
the future at a standstill;

you move freely between them both
to where the present
stretches on an infinite curve
upon which love now is fixed and
flowing without impediment,

for here lies something serious —
love at sixty-five;

you surprise your older self
with inward laughter,
smiling softly at a
younger him —

pulling the blinds down
against intrusion of prejudice,
light of experience.

Encounter With Chris The Fish

Can you give me
a plaice…
for two pounds?

you'll want me
to walk on water next –
he laughs…
I know my name's Chris
but…

I laugh…
don't worry,
it's small change
adding the 't'
if it helps?

Chuckling, he drops
a bagged fish
safely into my hand
for a couple of quid –

there's no water
for miles around.

Fly Music

Fly Music! Arch infinity and lift
To spheres I cannot reach
The inconsolable, the tears,
The rising sap
Trapped in its own flowering,
The breach of promise,
Rise with overpowering glory,
And a smiling backward glance
For I who made you dance,
Yet cannot tap my feet.
God knows from whence you came,
What beat, heartbeat
You claim exultingly to magnify –
Only release me from my longing,
Rinse my soul,
Surge from me, fill the sky
And leave me whole.

Remembering Michael

Michael Evans, 1964 – 1988, who died doing what he loved, mountaineering

How could I reach
into your world –
miraculous landscapes
netted in continents
as far apart
as heat and cold,
as light and dark?

You combed them
for shiny new experiences,
teasing out no bright pennies
but pockets full of pebbles
and bright flowers;
yours was a wild, a roving heart,
a towering mind –

and you were young –
and life was kind.

Parting should have been
visible to all,
but the shadow on
the mountain top tipped
time over, leaving us
with nothing but the rain –
like tears – and in the mist
one tall tree,
felled too soon.

Not Unsung

You were not unsung in my wild verses,
Often between the lines you crept,
Where thought fell like a shaft of light –
Or wept.

Gallows Hill Sunset

Warwickshire

Even the brown bird flying
across the amber light
of a setting sun not yet red
is, like the trunks of the trees,
burnt orange,
their dense, dark foliage
a fist of clubs
in the hill's still hand
until, one cloud shifts and,
under the dipping searchlight,
shadowed leaves become
burnt green,
one minute more and
all is shadow:

and now this hillside strip
of woodland waits resigned
for night to drift in
with piercing bark or shriek
of nocturnal beast,
the mellow t-whoo of owl,
grass parted with
padded feet running,
the tilted swoop of wing,
the grasp of jaw or beak
when earth has fully risen up
and dusk to dark declined.

A Song Of Freedom

Freedom is in the singing
not the song,
freedom is in the dancing
with the Spring,
freedom is understanding
thought not fact,
freedom is catching
wit upon the wing,
freedom is in the space
that laughter fills
between the devil
and the deep blue sea,
where with a little luck,
a little grace,
we see another as we
know ourselves to be:

freedom lives to die
a thousand deaths
in being thought so high
yet brought so low,
but still will rise again
and still inspire,
for every soul has
fetters that must go…

with freedom you believe
in what you will,
no shackled body
binds the mind that's free,
but for all the pain
or peace we sow,
death is the sweetest
freedom we shall know.

About the author

Maggie Goren was born in London in 1937 and educated at The City of London School for Girls. Much later in life she graduated from Oxford Brookes University in Art History, after a year studying anthropology with interest but no outcome. Across life Maggie was employed in the music industry in the U.K. and Australia and finally spent six years in the BBC TV News Division at Alexandra Palace and TV Centre as news typist, teleprompt operator and producer's secretary. In 1970 she married an Israeli engineer and in 1973 emigrated with two sons to Israel, arriving in time for the Yom Kippur War. After four years the family returned to the U.K.

Other poetry collections include *Hunchback & Clown* (1980) and *A Simple Easter* (2008), a handcrafted book of poetry illustrating the exquisite etchings of master-printer Michael Fell, which includes a CD of music by her son Dan and voice presentation by friend and actress, Sheila Probert.

An amusing and poignant travel autobiography, *Going Up, Going Down…The Aliyah of an Innocent…(Israel 1973 – 1977)* was published in 2011. A Selection of essays *Monthly Letters from Middle England* from a period over twenty years during which she edited a local magazine, should be appearing shortly. She also writes catalogue essays for the internationally renowned, New York abstract painter, Jeffrey Kroll.

Maggie's personal observations and philosophic musings follow their own road, whilst the author is swift to acknowledge a deep appreciation of Rilke, Pablo Neruda, Edna St. Vincent Millay, Norman Maccaig and Wislawa Szymborska particularly amongst countless other poets.

Maggie has four sons and currently lives in a rural village on the edge of the Cotswolds. Beyond writing, her other loves are family and friends, music, cooking and gardening.

www.maggiegoren.com

Maggie's illustrative collaborator, **Paul Eaton** brings all his experience and imagination to fully complementing the author's work, for which she is highly indebted and truly grateful.